Smack the dragon, Lou

erotic poetry

Carrie Fincher

ISBN 978-93-5610-054-1
© Carrie Fincher 2022
Published in India 2022 by Pencil

A brand of
One Point Six Technologies Pvt. Ltd.
123, Building J2, Shram Seva Premises,
Wadala Truck Terminal, Wadala (E)
Mumbai 400037, Maharashtra, INDIA
E connect@thepencilapp.com
W www.thepencilapp.com

DISCLAIMER: *The opinions expressed in this book are those of the authors and do not purport to reflect the views of the Publisher.*

Author biography

I have always been a writer.

I grew up in Germany, studied Italian Literature, Archeology and Geography, and at age 28 left everything behind to explore the world. For 11 years I drifted around, lived in Italy and Spain and Malaysia, and traveled to many other places, like Istanbul, Portugal, Mexico, Sri Lanka, India, California, Bali....

I seem to be a free spirit, maybe that is why lasting love has never found me.

This past year gave me poetry though, inspired by a beautiful man and amazing sex.

CONTENTS

a homage

I used to like writing poetry in school, but later lost interest. I felt poetry was cheesy and boring. But I guess I just read the wrong poetry?

But something happened in the summer of 2021. I met a man, and he unlocked a poetic flow that couldn't be stopped.

A writer, incredibly handsome (though not really my type at first sight actually), a traveler, intelligent, intellectual, a reader, slightly arrogant and self obsessed..and most of all: very dominant in bed.

I had carried those dark fantasies with me all my life, and never fully explored them. I had found my personal Fifty Shades of Grey (and my butt found many shades of black and blue). We only had a few meetings over the year but he left quite an impression on me. I got a crush for him - probably at the moment when he said "don't fall in love with me". Classic.

Anyhow, this is my little homage to wild sex and unfulfilled love. And to the words he gave me.

impression

and i am still feeling

that pressure on my chest

but only on the left side

it seems my heart has been compressed

it's been a wild night

we were exploring our lust

and i fell for you badly

because my heart just felt it must

and i couldn't feel myself

i could only feel the pain

i loved the way that you talked

and took me without shame

and now it seems

my heart is aching from your hands

but i think it simply knows

it's losing power to this man

but my head wants to stay free

as free as you are

but that pain in my chest

is a reminder so far

you'd made an impression on my heart literally

but despite thinking of you all the time i feel free

and i know i'm idealising

take me back to where i was

but no, i'm fantasizing

and i'm liking it so far

nothing wrong with imagining

a story to be told

when it feels so good and bad

it sure is worthy to unfold

choking

when i lay naked and choking

i communicate better

than with words spoken

at a dinner table

there is less vulnerability

in a stranger's intimacy

shrive

you didn't shrive

when i was on my knees

i'd confessed my sins

and i did say please

i had chased the passion

a taste of obsession

an unchaste mouth

a very good lesson

delusion of grandeur

you asked if i knew i was worth more

oh honey

the delusion of grandeur

i've been to places

you can't trace on maps

stitched one too many names

on my backpack

i stole, i took and put together

this person here under your leather

what is my own, where do i end

the borderline slipped out of hands

the floor i walk on soaking wet

you better tread careful on it

force

you are a force upon me

anything but boredom please

never understood the concept

of moderation or loneliness

all i have is honey

but you just want the white stuff

living your life in overdrive

and still never enough

there is a certain satisfaction in breaking hearts

that's why i want your desire

i need that dopamine rush

to get me higher

love making

my worth is holy

and i love to my limit

but i don't seem to belong

in nobody's hands

i don't understand

the concept of love

if you call it love making

can you make love in bed?

hands like water

your hands

your soft hands

like water moving through the night

where they fall

where they land

soft water at a waterfall

can crush stones over time

audacity

you had the audacity

finally somebody

to execute the deed

i didn't know was good or bad

for my head

but it had been a longing, a need

we never know if we regret

the things we never let

ourselves do, or feel, or live

until we try, receive and give

i don't regret i came to you

i might regret some things i wrote

although not really cuz they were true

and other people do

the same but would not tell

but i'm not playing games, that's not my style

and even though i fell

flat on my face again

i know after a while

i'm standing stronger than before

and now i just want more

so all i'm asking now is when

crossing the borderline

i thought i was prepared this time

i was ready to have you and lose you

but different story, different mind

new nuances of pain i never knew

i hardly know you so it wasn't far to fall

but i dove right in as i do and i gave my all

in delusion of grandeur, it seems a habit

i was running to the borderline, just to cross it

curious

i failed, i fucked up

but i needed to

cuz from the things we never do

we cannot ever fill our cup

you did fill my cup

and it overflowed

bottles up for too long

didn't know where to go

and your waters rinsed off

old stories and dust

and made the river flow again

cuz the heart said it must

you can beat me

but you can't beat my heart

it beats itself

take me back to the start

beauty is a privilege

beauty is a privilege

but can beauty birth depth

in the end all will fade

nothing stays

constant change

all impermanent

and nothing wrong with that

i found love in a crooked smile

i found love in old age

i found love, most of all

in music and sound

and intellect

i found love in beauty too

of course

we all do

i see people passing by

and wonder how they fell in love

and why

but maybe reason is not needed

for the heart to feed it

beauty is a privilege

but not required to match

a soul so deep

you lose yourself in it

earth girl

i am a weird mix of slut and shaman

earth girl trying to find healing

through the pain

any path is welcome

there is no shame

any path worth exploring

dreams of neon green vipers biting me

telling me to remove the poison in my life

your touch is the venom and the remedy

just cut me open with your knife

forest

i went as deep as i could

into the forest

looking for a way to get lost

swallowed by the soft ground underneath

the chorus from the song on repeat

some songs are not allowed to end

and from time to time i smelled

you in the mossy autumn leaves

sinking in

some tears of shame

i'd rather have you hit

me in the face

than say those words to me

but it was my fault

i asked for it

love again

i'll never love again

said the coward

i say

throw yourself in

dive deep

there is always reward

whiff of an easy prey

he took a whiff

he sniffed me out

and he knew

immediately

i was easy prey

i did my best

to pretend

that i didn't know

my worth

or lack thereof

i thought this time

i had confidence

that in was worthy to receive

a man like him

did i mention

i was easy prey

i played

along

and for a little while

i actually believed

believed that a girl like me

stood a chance

with a man like him

but all the time

he knew

we are being sent

the same teachers again and gain

until we learn

isn't it

and a good trigger

it was

brought up everything once again

the feelings

of utter unworthiness

the unloved child

became the unlovable woman

the voices in my head harsher

than any word he could ever spit at me

harder

than any lash he could ever give to me

i am my own worst enemy

self destruction at it's best

and the worst

is that he wasn't worth it

i never wanted him in the first place

but when got a whiff

of my special desires

i was easy prey

needless to say

i fell

defiantly

guess i just like pain

physically, psychologically

and psychedelically

maybe i'm losing my mind

but it's a good thing

Mooji would agree

you don't give me any hope no more

but let me worship

all your flaws

what a delusion

what an obsession

i tremble

but not in a good way

and i ache for your hand

my heart thrilled

for you still

impossibly

the audacity

atrocity

calling for mutiny

but i stand my ground

defiantly

joyously compromising

i think i want intimacy

i loved you sleeping next to me

you never know the things you miss

well you do know ignorance is bliss

i know and still i step

fully aware into the sticky trap

of idealizing fantasizing

joyously compromising

i hope you see

i'm only dramatizing

for the poetry

cuz who wants to be

with somebody

writing

about every item

of his or her history

naive's the heart

it is not smart

but at least it gives me

words and art

dance with you

dance with you

i want to dance with you

staring into

your eyes

raving through the night

high

those perfect times

until the sunrise

brings us down

back to the ground

arm in arm

after the storm

comes always the calm

art broken

art broken

those nights when gin

is soaking the pen

to write the story of my heart

right kind of wrong

you are the right kind of wrong to me

my favorite flavor

my chronic disease

i want to inhale

the smoke from your lungs

have your taste on my tongue

until you release me

again from your grip

so tight and so loosely

you would let me slip

out of your hands, out of your mind

distracted by cities, worlds and all kinds

right now i'm just grabbing the words out of this

an opportunity just too good to miss

cuz i don't know you and i'm not naive

i adore from afar, not looking to receive

i know it is wrong, wanting you near

butterflies should come from love, not from fear

roaming

you might envy my freedom to roam around

every night a new lover, i almost lost count

but don't be fooled, i always sleep alone

and when i call, nobody picks up the phone

but you're right, i cherish to be free

i am no possession and i can't possess thee

i would make me at home though

i could let it all go

i would stop all the roaming

because deep down i know

i long to nurture, to give and to care

to serve just one lover with whom i can share

this life, i'm looking for this gentleman

who knows how to love and how to be a man

a dirty mind with a golden heart

for him i would stop and for him i would start

to settle

or maybe we could roam together

guess i still have hopes in this thing called forever

and even if it won't last that long

i would give it my all, cuz my love is strong

but until then i rather be alone

than lonely with you

i'm not faking or pretending

to feel something that's not true

how can you expect me to fall in love

when i can't even fall asleep

in bed next to you

i am looking for arms to trust in

for arms i can keep

concubine

i dare

often a lot

but i do not really care

never bothered about etiquette

bored to be Wilde

i like to cross the line

free as a child

and naughty like a concubine

but that won't make me anybody's wife

men love the whore in bed

but not for life

it's sad

but seems to be a fact

that's why my bed stays cold after the act

re

that eager submissive body on the table

you can flip

sleep, breakfast, moral and honor

we can skip

that black silk stocking over my knee

you can rip

that last drop of wine from your palm

i will sip

waiting for the captain

returning with his ship

i want to drink his nectar

covered in his spit

oh sometimes

i want to cancel

my remembership

rock my boat

that rainy Sunday morning in August

a very strange match

worlds apart and still lots in common

no match at first sight i guess

didn't think i'd see him again

but he had thoughts of repetition

a gin soaked night

an English conversation

an interesting time between cushions

his beauty

standing in the doorway looking at me

his hair smelling of soap

touching my forehead

his long elegant perfect body

his carpet blood red

he is a good boy

with a very naughty side

he likes to write

in English most of all

distinguished wit and banter

and sexy notes at night

i hardly know him

but i must confide

he rocked my boat

like only few men might

he knows how to handle

he knows how to feed

my special desire

my special need

evergreen

oh honey i love your sugar

sweet stuff always lights me up

but your bitter taste on my tongue

crystals of bliss

i know there were many times

i crossed the line

it's paperthin

just like the line from

passion to obsession

or the addiction to sin

i'm just a flower in a pot

i guess i won't be growing up

but maybe you can add me to your window sill

next to the lines of books i will stand still

and wither slowly while you're crossing lines

to other countries cuz you're not mine

but i'm not like your other girls, i'm not an evergreen

i won't last long without a drop or fill in

hopes low

hopes low

but bodies rhyme

so

you reckon we have some time

to share

not looking for a life together

just for some lines to write and tear

cuz love's not linear

as we all know

so

let's write this verse, this poem, this song

and then we separate

if we don't get along

but if we do and our minds also entwine

if hopes get ignited and you wish to be mine

we might have a book or a record, a bestselling one

maybe just one, maybe some more to come

who knows, who can ever tell beforehand

that's why i keep my hopes low

for a soft ground to land

driftwood

it's not the same

i'm missing the pain

missing the muse

found no use

in hurting myself anymore

found happiness

through deconstruction

and there is not less

satisfaction in this

and even though your hands

caused too much damage

my body is craving the touch

it's never too much

and i float like damaged good

like driftwood

you're my favorite sweetest torture

my lust wants more

my head says blast it

no sense in skin black and blue

when the heart is searching for a different you

the table

drink me under the table

then fuck me on it

i am willing and able

oh boy you know it

we have to make time

for making love

i can be sublime

below and above

courage to surrender

it takes courage to surrender

to sit with the pain and deeply feel

it takes bravery to be tender

devotion is a special skill

who has the power, who is in charge

cuz i still hold my head up high

if the task to dominate is too large

i bend down low and spread my thighs

supervised fall

am i too much

or not enough

this body is craving your touch

is craving a love that's tough

and rough

like the rope around my thighs

you're pulling my strings

you're pulling my sighs

out of my lungs

out of my eyes

i freeze, i gasp, i bend

under control, under influence

your hot breath as you constrict

the flow of my blood, my oxygen, restrict

my precious freedom

i give you all

i need an alpha male

for a supervised fall

amano essere dominate, damn it

why do you still come to my dreams

asking for my birth date and time

spooning me from behind

can my mind

please finally comprehend

this has to end

i'm so over it

though apparently not

that flame got lit

my heart got shot

sorcerer

the beginning is always dark

and it's always darkest before the dawn

back when you left your first mark

and you moved me like yet another pawn

you travel between worlds and women

a modern Sir Richard Burton

while i'm just trying to find one man

for loving and for hurting

i could literally sit and write all day

you opened up everything needed to say

i sway

under your gaze

your eyes they do amaze

estimate my worth

expand my girth

let me give birth

to worlds of words and foreign language

you are the sorcerer, i am the witch

rough nights

the rough nights after Christmas

in your bed there is

a canyon

between us as we slept

grabbed and tossed around

between sheets and cushions

i don't know my way out

and i know you're not mine

but that's why i chose you

with lips so blue from wine

that don't say nothing that's not true

shall we just say

you are a sweet torture

and a bitter remedy

i am craving my medicine

but self love is self discipline

adoration

i'll wait till you're gone again

to express my deep adoration

so that you won't draw away

while you're still here

and i hope you will read my poems

in the way i meant them

so that when you come home

you might be inspired to fathom

wishful thinking maybe

cuz in the end it's just my words

and you ain't looking for a baby

you're just slipping hands under skirts

please don't take too serious

every syllable i write

i'm just trying to stay gracious

in your beautiful bright light

union

i love when you

leave a trace of yourself

inside of my body

your dna

from a rush of excitement

a drop in the ocean

when two bodies bend

a sacred potion

union

confess

confess

and then undress

i can be forgiving

like Jesus

explore

the writer

the beautiful traitor

is he making me sick

is he part of the cure

all i know is i want to explore

interrupt a detonation

and would i really want to be your girl

i am worried i will bore

you cuz my intellect

has gaps

my wit and humour

can be wrapped

up in a single night

and then what's left

why would you stay

i look at other people wondering what they say

to each other after all those years

how does love work

when love so often ends in tears

in disappointed expectations

you cannot interrupt a detonation

is monogamy just a beautiful construct

and love at first sight really is just lust

so isn't it better not to burn the fuse

and just be present right here

right now

with my beautiful muse

cuz i'm making up stories in my head

not everything thought needs to be said

a drug's a drug

thank you for the inspiration

thank you for that release

thank you for the fascination

not hesitating in my wish to please

i didn't think i had

an addictive personality

but a drug's a drug

and thankfully

my drug is often out of reach

which gives me time to rearrange

to clear my body and my mind

because i know that each

return will easily find

me back in overindulgence

withdrawal not an easy feat

you cannot forever keep

the drug out of your thoughts, put on a shelf

it has wrapped itself tightly around myself

and life in rehab is all bland

i miss that smile, i miss that hand

reverse

losing myself and self respect

thinking it is love

but that is how an addict acts

when she wants the drug

i really should know better

how to protect myself

raise the anchor, close the shutter

put the gear into reverse

i can be so light, aloof and fun

but some days i am none

of the above

then i just need love

like a charm

he told me not to fall in love

so i didn't

worked very well

like a charm

cuz you can tell

the heart to stop feeling

what it shouldn't

why i wanted you

i didn't want you at first

you'd only quenched my thirst

i didn't want you at the start

there was no bit that touched my heart

you were too smooth, too arrogant

though not a bad mid morning in the end

didn't consider meeting again

but then

when i discovered

intellect and beauty coming together

your words, your book

a man not only of good looks

a strong and gentle side that left me weak

grew into something i would seek

and when i knew i couldn't have it

my old bad habits

kicked in

leading me onto thin

ice

twice

thrice

that's how addiction starts i guess

and then you wonder how you could ever live with less

i might exaggerate

it's just something i'd like to state

here in my words and rhymes

sometimes

i wish i could be

just like the others and fall happily

in love

but i don't seem to allow myself that bliss

cuz even happiness

gets boring after a sweet while

that's why i love and go down in style

and free forever more

washed down a different shore

but let me just state it here once more

i like you much, you opened a door

another spectrum of my personality

another chapter of the road

maybe you don't want me

maybe you just want to stay free

nothing promised, nothing owed

it's not an issue

you came out of the blue

and i know i did ignore the cue

you were something surprisingly new

and that is why i wanted you

that which is a heart

you say

the heart shall be protected

but how

i had erected

a wall so high

equipped with barb wire

and still your words did plough

right through

your gaze found cracks in my defense

my armor didn't stand a chance

my heart defeated by you

you were so right, i cannot fake

that which is a heart, that can break

smack the dragon, Lou

he must be tired of being adored

bored

by all the girls falling

he cannot bother, it's rather appalling

he can have them all but what is he looking for

a wanderer, a searcher

arrogance and confidence

no chance

to escape that sex appeal

and feel

that dark necessity

smack the dragon, Lou

i know you want to

you are sublime

very well defined

but let me check your vital sign

while i am starving

carving

your love

out of my ribs

and sipping red wine from your fingertips

beautify reality

when i love

i fully love, no limit

romanticize you in my head

create a person in it

that probably does not exist

but that is what love is for

to live in bliss

and beautify

reality